www.alysbooks.com

Your Book | Our Mission

Cooking with Miss Jade

First Edition 2014
Published by Aly's Books

www.alysbooks.com
Your Book | Our Mission

Edited by Irrefutable Proof
www.irrefutable-proof.com

Designed by Fish Biscuit

ISBN: 970 0 9941767 4 5

This book is dedicated to my grandmother, Nana Brustolin. My grandmother and I had a close relationship and enjoyed creating together in the kitchen. Some cakes were burnt, others exploded, and we always made a good mess together.

A big thank you to my husband David for all the fantastic ideas and inspiration while creating this book. You have been my support from day one when I started writing this book. Thank you for taste testing all my new recipes.

The creative artwork by Ella Rasmussen and Roree Taylor is amazing. Together they have created the perfect drawings to fit this cookbook, and I look forward to working with them again for my next book.

Thank you to Jade Llamas from UnJaded Design and Photography. It has be a wonderful experience working with you and I hope to work with you in years to come.

Thank you to all the children and families with whom I have worked in childcare. You have been an inspiration for family cooking.

And finally, my support crew of friends who have stuck by me during this time – Georgia Lysaght, Kirree Jenkings, Fleur Balmain, Amber Wilson, Laine Taylor and Louise and Larni Rasmussen.

I hope you enjoy the adventure as much as I have!

Happy cooking

So why Miss Jade?

I have worked as a preschool teacher, a nanny and a ski instructor, and since my first day at work up to this very day my colleagues, customers, friends and family call me Miss Jade.

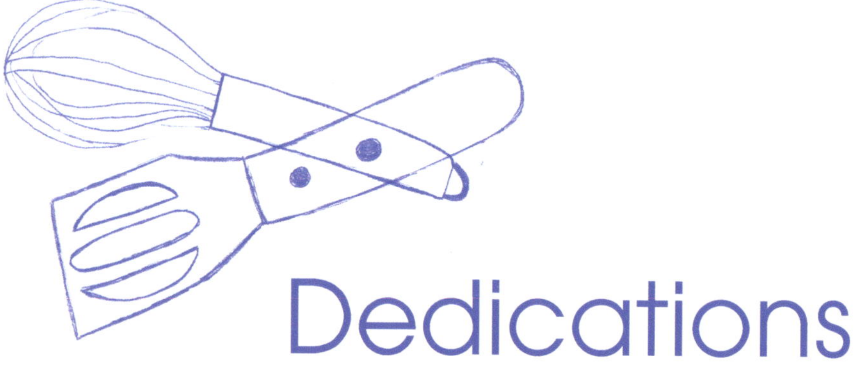

Dedications

Sir Trent Madsen from Kinetic Martial Arts, Sutherland Shire N.S.W Australia.

Angela Keel – Blue M Food Co, Sydney N.S.W Australia

Nicole Pavett – Supernova ME. WWW.supernovame.com.au

Barbara Greve, USA.

Uncle John and Aunty Marilyn

The Tarrant family

Jenny Wilson

Julie-Ann Martinovich

Sky Barnes

Colin Mulhall – Southern Fasteners Kirrawee, Sydney Australia

Lynn Drummond

Nathan Green of Coffeelichious Mobile

Isa and JP Chartier

Gloria Gallardo-Walker

Contents

Introduction

While I was growing up I loved to spend time with my grandmother. Most of all, I enjoyed cooking with her in her little kitchen in Monterey, Sydney, Australia.

My mother and grandmother have been my biggest inspirations when it comes to cooking. They always had their own special touch while they were making their delicious creations. I'm proud to say I have inherited their flair and love for cooking.

By the age of 9 I was unstoppable in a kitchen – roasting lamb, making rissoles by hand, whipping smooth, creamy mash, creating herb-infused spaghetti bolognese, baking delicious banana bread and much more for my family to enjoy.

By 18, I was incredibly curious about the food of different cultures, so I uprooted myself from Sydney and set out to see the world. I travelled the world by myself and experienced so many different flavours from so many destinations. I tasted food and collected recipes from places such as Thailand, Italy, USA, Canada and China (to name a few favourites!).

However, during my travels I experienced an unknown, on-going illness. During 2002, while in the USA, I suffered an extreme allergic reaction and was rushed to hospital.

I was informed then that I have a severe intolerance to gluten known as Crohn's Disease, and I was also diagnosed with Ulcerative Colitis.

As hard as it was, from that day on I had to change my diet dramatically and eliminate all gluten.

I was bitterly disappointed that there were so many things I would not be able to enjoy again! But I persevered; I knew I could not let Crohn's Disease get the best of me, and I recreated every single recipe in my collection. I want to share all of the recipes that I have gathered with my family, friends, and the world. All of my recipes are my own or special family dishes that we have created together and are happy to share with you in this book.

These gluten free meals have given me a much healthier and happier lifestyle. It has opened my eyes and taste buds to the wonderful culinary world, and made me realise that healthy food does not have to be boring!

Today, I find myself sitting with my husband in Thailand where I first started to explore different kinds of food and the spice of life. My husband shares my passion for cooking, and we work well together as we try out new recipes in our kitchen in Southern Sydney.

Some children enjoy helping in the kitchen, and this is the perfect collection of recipes for your children to help you with.

When you have family and friends calling around on the weekends and you need something quick to whip together, grab this book and start cooking.

This collection is also handy for children's birthday parties, with many yummy treats to share with their friends.

I hope you enjoy my spice of life.

Happy cooking!

Important information

Always seek advice from your GP if you experience any allergic reactions to food.

Children must be supervised by an adult at all times whilst in the kitchen.

While creating this book some products, ingredients and packaging may have changed. Please read all food labels when shopping for products, as it will be stated on the packaging whether the product is gluten free, or contains ingredients such as nuts and dairy products.

Adapting to living with food allergies

This book is a guide to help you change your everyday diet to a gluten free or food allergy sensitive diet.

Changing your diet can be quite challenging, even when it comes to taking away one ingredient such as gluten. Cooking meals for the family at home can be challenging in itself.

This book will allow you to swap and change the recipes so they can be adjusted to your dietary requirements, including soy products, no nuts, vegetarian, gluten or dairy free.

Gluten sensitivity and intolerance has been recognised by many people, and most people with Ulcerative Colitis, Celiac or Crohn's disease are forced to omit gluten from their diet.

I'm happy to say I eat a clean gluten free diet and I no longer need to take medication for my Crohn's and Ulcerative Colitis disease. I feel much better and have lots of energy to live my life to the fullest.

Some of the main reasons people give up wheat, dairy and nut products are because they have an intolerance or allergy to the foods they are eating.

Some of the side effects experienced may be:

- Diarrhoea or constipation
- Bloated stomach
- Gas
- Pains in the stomach
- Swelling and redness of the eyes
- Rash around the neck and face
- Redness and swelling in the face
- Swelling of the tongue and lips
- A runny nose
- A restless sleep at night

These are only some of the side effects that can occur with food allergies.

Things to look out for that may contain gluten that you may not know about include:

- Bread
- Pizza base
- Pasta
- Wheat
- Rye
- Barley
- Some soups
- Breadcrumbs
- Flour
- Soy sauce
- Seasoning mixtures
- Chips with seasoning
- Frozen chips

- Apple/fruit pie
- Some ice creams
- Cheesecake
- Some chocolate mousse
- Marinades on meat
- Some coffee
- Some salad dressings
- Some alcohol
- Some deep fried foods with batters

On the brighter side of things, foods that are gluten free include:

- Rice flour
- Rice crumbs
- Corn flour
- Eggs
- Natural yoghurt
- Plain nuts and seeds
- Pure oils
- Sugar
- Honey
- Rice noodles
- Fresh meat and fish
- Fresh vegetables and fresh fruit
- Fresh herbs grown from your garden at home

I hope you enjoy the book, and happy cooking!

Whilst growing up, my mother and grandmother were fantastic teachers in the kitchen. They always included me when they were cooking and nurtured my love for homemade food.

My grandmother never followed recipes in cookbooks and Mum always put her own twist on the finished product.

Today, cooking in my own kitchen, I love to experiment with different herbs and spices to create my own dishes.

All my recipes are homemade and I enjoy using fresh produce from my vegetable and herb garden in my dishes. I have put together a few of my favourite ingredients in creating this cookbook, and I hope you enjoy it.

Honey

When using honey in my recipes, I always try and support local beekeepers in Sydney and along the South Coast of Sydney. Fresh honey is always a better option to cook with. If you can find raw organic honey in your health food stores this is also a nice option.

Oil

When a recipe calls for cooking oil I like to use olive oil, avocado oil or chilli oil, to give added flavour to the finished product. From experience I have found avocado oil and chilli oils at markets, cooking shows, organic health food shops and on occasion at the local supermarket. You have to keep an eye out for these products as they can sell out fast!

Blue M Food Co.

Blue M Food products are rich, luscious and bursting with flavour. They remain handmade, preservative free and gluten free. You can find them in gourmet food stores throughout Australia and online. Their products include jams, chutneys and a range of smoked nuts. The sour cherry jam is my favourite, on a piece of gluten free toast in the morning with a cup of tea – DELICIOUS!

Blue M Food Co can be found at www.bluemfood.com

Cracked black pepper

I love using cracked black pepper in most of my recipes; I believe it is one of the best ways to enhance flavour in food. It's better to start with a small twist of pepper rather than over doing it at the start. Keep tasting your dish during cooking to get the flavour to your liking.

Fresh herbs from the garden

Fresh herbs are the best ingredients to cook with, and I much prefer to grow my own at home. The herbs and spices I like the most are coriander, chives, rosemary, Thai basil, chilli, garlic, garlic chives and spring onions.

Fresh home grown avocado

I enjoy using my grandfather's fresh home grown avocados, picked from the tree growing in his back yard. A fresh home grown avocado, or one picked up from a local farmer, will always taste better and last longer. I find when you need to ripen an avocado it's best placed with bananas in natural light.

Gluten free fettuccine pasta

When using pasta products in some of my recipes I prefer to use gluten free fettuccine pasta. The fettuccine pasta holds its shape better than other pastas I have tried, and when boiling it doesn't turn to mush.

When boiling your pasta it can take around 8 to 10 minutes to cook. After draining, give it a good rinse with hot water. If you are unsure, follow the directions on the pack, as the manufacturer will have suggested cooking instructions for the type of pasta you choose.

A few secrets for general health and wellbeing...

Kinetic Martial Arts

Kinetic Martial Arts is a place of health, strength and fitness. Most of all they have a strong focus on the positive development of each and every member.

The dedicated martial art instructors take the time to support you in every way possible, from training on the mats to everyday life coaching. You feel like family as soon as you walk in the door, and they take great pride in being a part of your journey.

A quote from Sir Trent Madsen 'Chief Instructor' that I always keep in mind is:

"Life is an interesting journey with twists and turns, peaks and valleys. Everybody walks though my door for different reasons. Everybody has an interesting journey in life and I feel so privileged to be a part of it and I thank you for taking this step. I like to fill my Dojang with happy positive people and when you surround yourself with positive people you live your life to the fullest."

Whilst training at Kinetic Martial Arts I have taken the biggest step in my life to improve my health and fitness. This has helped me control my Crohn's disease and Ulcerative Colitis, while feeling better within myself.

Visit Kinetic Martial Arts at www.kineticmartialarts.com.au

Embrace

Embrace is a favourite shop that I often visit, located in Westfield Miranda (Sydney NSW). Embrace features meditation workshops, psychic readings, psychic café nights, healings, books on healthy living, support and advice for your everyday life. Rosie from Embrace organises a festival each year that is held in Sydney called the Festival of Dreams. This is a hub of education on living a healthier life, such as gluten free foods, cleansing and detox, healings, Chakra balancing workshops and seminars. If you're in the area stop in and have a chat with Rosie and her staff down at Embrace and enjoy the positive energy that puts the bounce back in your day. You can find my book Cooking with Miss Jade at Embrace, or visit them at www.embraceaustralia.com.au

Spiritual Healing House

One place I enjoy visiting is the Spiritual Healing House in Queensland. The Spiritual Healing House offers healing workshops, healings and massage. People travel from all around the world to visit Linda. As Linda tells me, "Most people who visit me at the Spiritual Healing House are gluten intolerant". It's been a delight to spend time with Linda in the kitchen, and now she bakes yummy gluten free treats for her visitors. It's always a delight to visit Linda at the Eumundi markets, on Wednesdays and Saturdays. If you're in the area drop in to have a quick chat or have a life-changing healing session in the great outdoors.

Eumundi in QLD

Eumundi Markets is a must-do for gluten free products. You can find anything from cakes, sandwiches, quiches, slices, fresh fruit and vegies. Many of the main ingredients in this cookbook can be found here.

Merry Beach

Merry Beach is a hidden place on the NSW South Coast where you can camp in a tent or park your caravan at the beachfront. Around the area there are many rustic places to go fishing, bushwalking and just relax. A favourite pastime of mine is campfire cooking; slow roasting a leg of lamb with vegetables would be one of my all time favourite things to cook over the campfire. An old time treat is jacket potatoes wrapped in foil and slowly roasted in the hot coals in the bottom of the campfire, served with melted cheese, chives and bacon on top. For something sweet, try roasted banana served with gluten free choc chips and ice cream to go on top!

I hope you enjoy this collection of recipes for children and families who have food allergy issues. I hope that it raises awareness about Ulcerative Colitis, Celiac disease, irritable bowel syndrome, Crohn's disease and healthier living.

Cooking with Children

Cooking in the kitchen with children can be a fun 'hands on' experience, where children can become aware of food handling and safety in the kitchen.

This can help children get excited about healthy eating, and get them packing their own lunch box to take to school each day.

Cooking together can provide many learning opportunities whilst creating a fantastic mess!

Here are a few safety tips for cooking with children:

- Adult supervision at all times
- The child should always ask an adult for permission before they start cooking
- Wash and dry hands before cooking
- Tie long hair back before children start cooking
- Use an apron while cooking
- When using a cooking pot or fry pan, turn the handle to the back of the stove so you don't knock the handle and spill your food, or worse, scald a child
- Supervise children while using sharp knives
- Use a chopping board when cutting ingredients (Not the kitchen bench!)
- Don't forget to put the lid back on bottles after you have used them
- Always use oven gloves when moving your dish into and out of the oven
- Have a dry tea towel handy
- Use the oven light to have a look into the oven, and be careful of the outside of the oven as it can be hot
- When using a microwave, remember to use a microwave safe dish and cover food with a paper towel or microwave safe cover
- After filling up the sink to do the washing up, turn the tap to cold and run a small amount of water out of the tap. This prevents a child burning their hands after you have used the tap

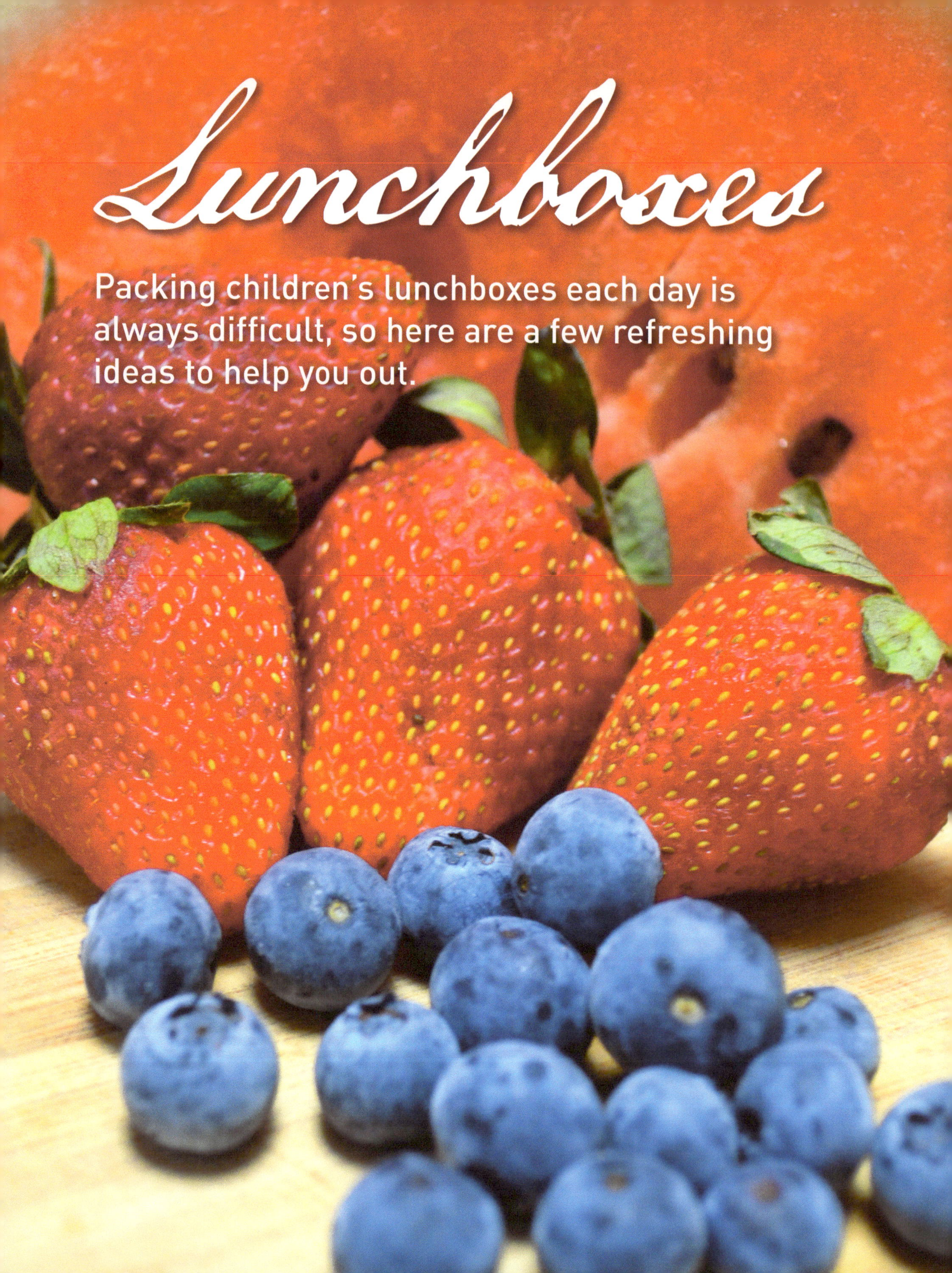

Lunchboxes

Packing children's lunchboxes each day is always difficult, so here are a few refreshing ideas to help you out.

Lunch box tips

When packing a lunch box don't forget school is a nut free zone, so don't pack peanut butter, muesli bars with nuts, or raw or loose nuts.

When packing sandwiches into lunch boxes use a cookie cutter such as butterfly, car, dolphin, star, flower, fish or love heart to make your child's lunch box exciting.

You can also cut the sandwich into 3 strips with the crust cut off, making it easier to eat them quickly so they can join their friends at play.

When you're packing lunch boxes use colourful foods so when your child opens it up it looks inviting.

When it's hot, freeze a popper and use it as an ice brick in the lunch box. If you place it in a zip lock bag it won't leak onto the food. The zip lock bag can be used as a rubbish bag if needed. You can also pack a flat ice brick to keep the lunch box cold.

It sometimes helps to put a little note in your child's lunch box with a happy message or a funny drawing to brighten up their day.

A 'sometimes' treat can be banana bread. This can be toasted in a flat sandwich press to make it warm. Wrap in foil or seal tight in a container to keep it a little warm until morning tea time.

Some other tasty treats are carrot cake, gluten free pancakes with jam, ham and cheese cupcakes and gluten free apple chocolate chip muffins.

Healthy snacks can include:

- Guacamole dip with rice crackers and cheese
- Cucumber or carrot sticks with beetroot dip
- Carrot sticks or apple slices with hummus dip
- Rice crackers with cheese
- Fruit salad with yoghurt
- Frozen grapes
- Homemade fruit balls
- Gluten free wrap with cheese and ham
- Crumbed chicken and cheese in a gluten free wrap
- Gluten free pita bread with chicken, cheese and mayonnaise
- Dried apples
- Dried bananas
- Blueberries in a small container

If you have a fussy eater, packing a selection lunch box is a good idea for them. They can pick at whatever they feel like: cherry tomatoes, cucumber sticks, olives, cheese, a rolled up slice of ham or salami, rice crackers, dried bananas, yoghurt and cucumber, peeled mandarin, banana bread, blueberries and puffed rice cracker thins.

When children get home from school they are always looking for a treat to munch on before dinner. A selection of the above items is always great for this.

Side Dishes and Starters

Uncle John's Potato Salad

Serves 4 people

Ingredients

500g mini white potatoes
2 spring onions
½ small brown onion
5 rashers short cut smoky bacon
Cracked black pepper
Dry Italian mixed herbs
1 tablespoon fresh coriander
Whole egg mayonnaise
½ teaspoon crushed garlic
Soft butter

Equipment

Medium size pot
Non-stick small fry pan
1 medium-sized serving bowl
Chopping board
Teaspoon
Tablespoon
Wooden spoon

Step 1. Fill large cooking pot half full with water and bring to boil. Chop all potatoes into quarters and place into boiling water. Cook on high for 10 to 15 minutes.

Step 2. Dice all the bacon and half a brown onion into small squares. Cook at a high heat for 5 minutes in a small non-stick fry pan, stirring constantly and seasoning with a pinch of cracked black pepper and a pinch of mixed herbs. Cook until golden brown then remove from the heat and set aside.

Step 3. Chop 1 tablespoon of coriander and 2 spring onions, then place half of each into a serving bowl. Add to the serving bowl ½ teaspoon of crushed garlic, a pinch of cracked black pepper, a pinch of mixed herbs, 1 teaspoon of butter, and half of the cooked bacon and brown onions.

Step 4. After the potatoes are cooked, drain the water and place the potatoes into the serving bowl. Add 2 tablespoons of mayonnaise, the rest of the spring onions, coriander, bacon and brown onion. Then mix all together.

Quick tip: You can serve this dish hot or cold, and it compliments a BBQ or nice Christmas seafood lunch well. If you need to make a larger serving, add more potatoes and season to taste.

If you would like to make a vegetarian version, remove the bacon.

Amber's Potato Bake

Serves 6 people

Ingredients

1 teaspoon gluten free minced garlic
4 spring onions
10 large potatoes
Cracked black pepper
Dried mixed herbs
300ml thickened cream
600g grated mozzarella cheese
4 rashers short cut bacon
Butter

Equipment

Chopping board
Teaspoon
Peeler
Small non-stick fry pan
Large rectangular casserole dish with lid

Note: Preheat your oven to 200C before you start cooking and grease the casserole dish with butter and set aside.

Step 1. Dice bacon into small squares and cook in a fry pan for 3 to 5 minutes on medium heat, then set aside to cool. In the base of the casserole dish place 1 teaspoon of gluten free minced garlic, a pinch of dried mixed herbs and a pinch of cracked black pepper.

Step 2. Peel and slice the potatoes thinly and dice the spring onions. Place a layer of sliced potato in the base of the casserole dish, then garnish with spring onions, bacon, dried herbs, cracked black pepper and a small amount of grated cheese. Repeat this step one more time.

Step 3. After you have made two layers of potato, place the last layer of potato on top and pour the thickened cream on, covering all of the potatoes. Sprinkle grated cheese evenly over the top, covering all of the potatoes. You should leave 1 inch from the top so the cheese won't boil over the sides of the casserole dish and burn. Place into the oven for 1 hour and check after 30 minutes.

To test if your potato bake is cooked, remove from oven and place on a heatproof surface. Pierce the potatoes with a sharp knife, and if they're soft, your potato bake is ready.

Allow to cool for 10 minutes and it's ready to serve.

Dave's BBQ Chicken Skewers

Serves 2 people

Ingredients

500g chicken breast
2 tablespoons fresh honey
2 tablespoons gluten free soy sauce
1 tablespoon gluten free oyster sauce
1 teaspoon gluten free minced garlic
Cracked black pepper
Mixed herbs
Bamboo skewers

Equipment

Chopping board
Tablespoon
Teaspoon
Large rectangular container with lid
Medium size mixing bowl

Step 1. Slice chicken breast into long thin strips roughly 2-3cm thick, then using the spiked end thread the chicken onto the bamboo skewer. You should be able to make around 10 chicken skewers. Repeat steps until you have used all the chicken. When threading the chicken onto the skewer only push the skewer ¾ of the way into the chicken so you don't have the spike coming out the other end of the chicken.

Step 2. Place chicken skewers into the large rectangular container, place lid on top and set aside. In a medium size mixing bowl combine 1 tablespoon of gluten free oyster sauce, 2 tablespoons of gluten free soy sauce, 2 tablespoons of fresh honey, 1 teaspoon of gluten free minced garlic, 1 teaspoon of mixed herbs, 2 pinches of cracked black pepper, mixing together.

Step 3. Pour the mix over the chicken skewers, rolling the chicken around in the mix so they are fully coated. Place lid on top and refrigerate for an hour to marinate.

Step 4. After 1 hour remove from refrigerator and heat up BBQ plate. When the plate is heated, place the chicken skewers on the BBQ and start cooking. You will need to cook them for 15 to 20 minutes, turning constantly and basting with the left over marinade.

Step 5. When the chicken is cooked the meat will be white on the inside. Remove from the BBQ and cool for 5 minutes before serving.

Quick tip: Chicken skewers are great to serve with gluten free sweet chilli sauce, mango chutney, sour cream and smoky BBQ sauce.

Aunty Marilyn's Fried Rice

Serves 8 people

Ingredients

1 cup cooked white rice
6 strips smoky bacon (rind on)
6 spring onions
½ a red capsicum
½ a green capsicum
5 large stalks of celery
2 eggs
½ cup frozen corn
½ cup frozen peas
1 tablespoon gluten free soy sauce
Oil
Cracked black pepper
1 teaspoon dried Italian mixed herbs

Equipment

1 measuring cup
1 non-stick small or medium saucepan
Non-stick wok
Large mixing bowl
Small mixing bowl
Chopping board
Wooden spoon
Tablespoon
Large serving dish

Note: You will need to cook 1 cup of white rice and place in the fridge overnight in an air-tight container. Alternatively, you can use the cooked rice after it has cooled for a minimum of 15 minutes.

Cooking the rice

Place 1 cup of white rice into a non-stick saucepan and add 2 cups of water. Place on stovetop and set element to high heat.

Once the water has started to warm, stir regularly and bring to the boil. Once the rice has reached boiling point and the water has started to evaporate turn down to a low heat for 5 minutes, keeping a close eye on it as stirring may be required.

After 5 minutes remove from the heat and allow to cool.

Quick tips

- Spring onions – use the bottom half, the white to green area of the spring onion
- Celery – use the brighter green area of the celery
- Gluten free soy sauce – it's best to start with adding small amounts, adding more depending on your taste as you go

Options

- If you don't like spring onions, you can use one large brown onion chopped and cooked until golden brown to match your taste buds
- Left over Christmas ham is a great option, or you can use honey ham
- You can make this vegetarian fried rice if needed by removing the meat from the recipe
- Eggs are optional as it depends on the dietary requirements

Step 1. Whisk 2 eggs in a bowl. Place a small amount of oil in the wok and set on a high heat.

Step 2. Pour the whisked eggs into the heated work and lightly cook to create an omelette, flipping once and cooking each side evenly. Once cooked, remove from wok and place on a plate. When cooled cut into small strips and set aside.

Step 3. Turn wok down to a medium heat and dice the bacon (with the rind left on) into small chunks. Dice half a brown onion into small pieces. Gently cook the bacon and onion for 2 minutes and season with a pinch of cracked black pepper and a teaspoon of mixed dried herbs.

Step 4. After dicing the spring onions, capsicum and celery add them to the wok and cook for 2 minutes. After 2 minutes add the corn and peas then cook for a further 5 minutes.

Step 5. Add the rice and eggs, and stir in 1 tablespoon of gluten free soy sauce to taste. Cook for 2 to 3 minutes and stir when needed. Remove from heat and place into a large serving dish, cool for 5 minutes, and your rice is ready to serve.

Georgia's Spinach and Feta Salad

Serves 4 people

Ingredients

200g washed spinach leaves
100g fresh feta cheese
1 punnet fresh washed cherry tomatoes
1 tin (450g) of chickpeas, washed
1 small sweet potato
Gluten free Moroccan seasoning
Dried mixed herbs
Olive oil

Optional extra - walnuts or thinly sliced almonds

Equipment

Chopping board
Small fry pan
Medium fry pan
Small microwave safe bowl
Small bowl
Teaspoon
Wooden spoon
Colander
Large salad bowl (to serve)

Step 1. Wash and drain spinach leaves and place into large salad bowl. Wash and drain the cherry tomatoes and add to the salad bowl.

Step 2. Gently wash the chickpeas in a colander and rest in the sink to drain all the water. Heat the medium fry pan on high heat and drizzle a small amount of olive oil into the fry pan to heat. When the pan is hot, add the chickpeas and 1 teaspoon of Moroccan seasoning. Cook for 1 minute, constantly moving the chickpeas around the pan. Remove from heat and place into a small bowl to rest and cool.

Step 3. Peel sweet potatoes and chop into small rough chunks. Place them into a microwave safe bowl and warm in the microwave for 2 minutes. Remove from microwave and drain excess water if needed. Heat a drizzle of olive oil in a small fry pan on high. Once hot, add the sweet potatoes and 2 pinches of dried mixed herbs. Cook for 2 minutes, constantly moving the sweet potato around the pan. Remove from fry pan and place in a dish to cool.

Step 4. Crumble feta cheese into the salad bowl, add the cooled chickpeas and sweet potatoes, and toss salad with salad tongs. Your salad is ready to serve.

Quick tip: If you like salad dressing you can serve this dish with a vinaigrette. This salad is a great accompaniment for chicken skewers, BBQ steak and roast salmon.

Dad's Four-Layer Dip

Serves 10 people

Ingredients

250ml light sour cream
3 large avocados
1 lemon
Cracked black pepper
Salt
1 small block of tasty cheese (or your preferred cheese)
300g gluten free salsa
Gluten free Tabasco sauce

Equipment

Medium mixing bowl
Small mixing bowl
Wooden spoon
Teaspoon
Tablespoon
Chopping board
Grater
Glass pie dish

Step 1. Pour sour cream into the medium mixing bowl, add one twist of pepper, 3 drops of Tabasco sauce and mix together with a tablespoon. Set aside.

Step 2. Cut open avocados, remove stones and scoop out avocado flesh into a small mixing bowl then mash together. While mashing the avocados add a squeeze of lemon, a pinch of salt and 2 pinches of pepper. Place avocado filling in pie dish, spreading evenly over the base of the dish.

Step 3. Pour sour cream mixture gently over the avocado layer and spread evenly.

Step 4. Pour salsa gently over the sour cream layer and spread evenly.

Step 5. Grate desired amount of cheese and sprinkle over the top.

Quick tip: Great options to this serve with are, gluten free rice crackers, gluten free corn chips, gluten free pita bread, cucumber sticks or carrot sticks.

This dip is fantastic to share with friends at a BBQ or a nice starter to tide over hungry family and friends. This dip serves around 15 people, and you will need lots of chips, bread, crackers and vegetable sticks to serve, as you will run out quickly.

Kirree's French Dip

Serves 4 people

Ingredients

1 packet French onion gluten free soup mix
1 container (250ml) light sour cream
1 small lemon
Cracked black pepper
1 spring onion

Equipment

Medium mixing bowl
Small wooden spoon
Chopping board

Step 1. Pour the sour cream into the mixing bowl and mix with a wooden spoon until soft.

Step 2. Mix the gluten free French onion soup mix into the sour cream and set aside.

Step 3. Chop the spring onion into small slices and mix into the sour cream.

Step 4. Cut the lemon in half. Squeeze in juice to taste. Add two pinches of cracked black pepper to the mixture and combine.

Step 5. Pour the dip into a serving bowl and it is ready to serve.

Quick Tip: Serve with gluten free rice crackers, carrot sticks, cucumber sticks, gluten free pita bread or roasted/toasted corn wraps.

This dip is fantastic to share with friends at a BBQ

Lynn's Gluten Free Salmon and Cream Cheese Wraps

Makes 4 wraps

Ingredients

Gluten free corn wraps
100g sliced smoked salmon
Chive and garlic cream cheese
Cracked black pepper

Equipment

Chopping board
Serving plate

Step 1. Warm a gluten free corn wrap in the microwave for 15 seconds. Remove and place onto a chopping board. Spread chive and garlic cream cheese onto the corn wrap with a teaspoon and season with cracked black pepper.

Step 2. Place smoked salmon on top of the cream cheese and roll the wrap, then cut in half. Repeat steps 1 and 2 until all the smoked salmon has been used.

Quick tip: If you're sending the wrap as a lunch box snack, wrap tightly in foil and place an ice brick in the lunch box. Dipping sauce options are mayonnaise, hummus or guacamole dip.

Gracie's Guacamole Dip

Serves 6 people

Ingredients

2 avocados
1 small lemon
Salt
Cracked black pepper
1 small red onion
Minced garlic
1 small tomato

Equipment

Teaspoon
Chopping board
Large zip lock bag
Scissors
Small serving bowl

Step 1. Cut the onion in half. Dice one half into small cubes and place into bag. Add a pinch of salt, half a teaspoon of minced garlic and 2 pinches of cracked black pepper into the bag. Cut the lemon in half and squeeze a small amount of juice into the bag.

Step 2. Cut both avocados in half removing the avocado stone. Scoop the avocado flesh into the bag. Dice the tomato into small cubes and place in the zip lock bag.

Step 3. Close the zip lock bag and using your hands, mash the ingredients until mixed and most of the lumps are out.

Step 4. Cut a small corner off the bottom of the bag and squeeze out into a small serving bowl.

Quick tip: Serve with gluten free rice crackers, carrot sticks, cucumber sticks, gluten free pita bread or gluten free corn chips.

Lunch Box Tip: Guacamole dip is a healthy snack for children's lunch boxes. You will need to have an ice brick in the lunch box to keep it cold. Children like to eat guacamole dip with gluten free rice crackers, carrot sticks, cheese sticks and cucumber sticks.

Nulla's Grilled Halloumi

Serves 4 people

Ingredients

Halloumi cheese (250g)
Avocado oil
Minced garlic
Water

Equipment

Chopping board
Teaspoon
Tongs
Medium fry pan
Medium rectangular container

Step 1. Cut the halloumi into thin strips and place into the container with water. The water should cover all of the halloumi. Soak for 20 minutes.

Step 2. Drain the water from the container and set aside. Heat oil in fry pan on medium for around 3 minutes.

Step 3. Add half a teaspoon of minced garlic to the pan then add the halloumi and fry for 25 to 30 seconds on each side. After the halloumi has started to become crisp, remove from fry pan and cool for 2 minutes before serving.

Quick tip: Halloumi is great to serve with a nice salad, as finger food, as a side with a hot vegetarian breakfast or on a vegetarian club sandwich.

Guacamole dip is a healthy snack for children's lunch boxes.

Nan's Homemade Meatballs

Serves 6 people

Ingredients

300g minced beef
1 clove garlic
Cracked black pepper
Mixed Italian dried herbs
Olive oil
½ a small brown onion
1 tablespoon fresh coriander
Gluten free flour
Gluten free breadcrumbs
1 small egg

Equipment

Large mixing bowl
Tablespoon
Teaspoon
Fry pan

Step1. Place minced meat into a large mixing bowl and season with cracked black pepper. Add 2 pinches of dried mixed Italian herbs and combine. To the mixing bowl, add 1 tablespoon of finely chopped fresh coriander, 1 clove of chopped garlic, finely chopped brown onion, ½ a cup of gluten free bread crumbs and 1 small egg, and mix together for 1 minute.

Step 2. Using your hands and a teaspoon, spoon mixture into your hand. Roll your hands together to create a small ball and set aside. Repeat this step until all the mixture is used.

Step 3. Using a medium fry pan, warm a drizzle of oil on medium heat. While the pan heats, roll your meatballs in gluten free flour.

Step 4. Place the meatballs in the fry pan and cook on each side for 2 to 3 minutes. They should appear crispy and golden brown. Test them by cutting one open in the middle (it should not be pink).

Step 5. Remove from the fry pan and allow to cool for 5 minutes before serving.

Quick tip: Have tooth picks available to eat your meatballs with as it's so much easier to eat them this way rather than burning your fingers. It's nice to have gluten free sweet chilli sauce to dip them in, or smoky gluten free BBQ sauce

Tina's Fritters

Makes 14 fritters.

Ingredients

2 large potatoes (washed and peeled)
1 small egg
1 tablespoon gluten free corn flour
1 teaspoon mixed dried herbs
Cracked black pepper
1 tablespoon grated tasty cheese
1 tablespoon fresh coriander
1 spring onion
125g of sweet corn kernels (drained and washed)
Olive oil

Equipment

Large bowl
Teaspoon
Tablespoon
Peeler
Grater
Wok with drying rack
Chopping board

Step 1. Peel, wash and grate 2 potatoes on the chopping board and place in the large mixing bowl. Chop 1 tablespoon of fresh coriander and slice 1 spring onion, and place them in the mixing bowl.

Step 2. Add 1 tablespoon of gluten free cornflour, and 1 whisked egg to the mixing bowl and combine. Wash and drain 125g of sweet corn kernels and add to mixing bowl. Add 1 tablespoon of grated tasty cheese then season with cracked black pepper and 1 teaspoon of mixed herbs to taste.

Step 3. Add 1½ cups of olive oil to the wok and warm on high heat. When the oil is ready, take a scoop of the mixture in a tablespoon and press down on it using your other hand. Carefully add the fritter into the wok by placing it up against the side and slowly lowering it into the oil. The potatoes will start to fizz and cook. You will need to cook for 3 to 4 minutes, turning once. It's best to cook 4 to 5 fritters at a time, or as many as can fit in the wok without touching each other. Repeat until all the mixture used.

Quick tip: Potato fritters are best served with mango chutney, tomato chutney, gluten free sweet chilli sauce or gluten free smoky BBQ sauce.

You can serve as a starter or pack in a lunch box for a savoury treat. No matter how you serve them they will be eaten fast!

Main Meals

Pine Street Nachos

Serves 4 people

Ingredients

300g minced meat
200g gluten free corn chips
3 cups grated mozzarella cheese
2 tablespoons mild Moroccan seasoning
300g red kidney beans
1 fresh tomato
1 tablespoon tomato paste
¼ of a red capsicum
¼ of a green capsicum
½ of a brown onion
1 fresh ripe avocado
Lemon juice
Cracked black pepper
Sour cream

Equipment

Chopping board
2 Medium-sized bowls
Grater
Large fry pan
Pizza tray
Baking paper
Fork

Optional extra: Tomato salsa to serve on the side

Note: Before you start cooking preheat your oven to 200C. Wash the red kidney beans in a colander and drain over a sink. Line the pizza tray with baking paper and set aside.

Step 1. Heat fry pan over a high heat and add a small drizzle of oil. Dice ¼ red capsicum, ¼ green capsicum, ½ a brown onion and the tomato and set aside. Grate the cheese and place in a bowl ready to use.

Step 2. Once heated, add the mince to the fry pan and fry for 4 minutes. After 4 minutes add the onion and red and green capsicum, and fry for a further 2 minutes. Reduce the heat to low.

Step 3. Add 1 tablespoon of tomato paste, 2 tablespoons of Moroccan seasoning, diced tomato and the red kidney beans to the pan, stirring gently for 2 minutes. Turn off the heat.

Step 4. Place a handful of corn chips on to the baking tray and top with a sprinkle of grated cheese. Add the mince mixture to the middle of the tray, adding the rest of the corn chips and grated cheese on top. Place in the middle of the oven and bake for 8 minutes.

Step 5. Cut the avocado in half and de-stone. Scoop the avocado flesh into a bowl and mash. Add a twist of cracked black pepper and 5 drops of lemon juice to avocado. Continue mashing until smooth. After 8 minutes remove nachos from oven and place on a heatproof surface. Top with sour cream and mashed avocado.

Your nachos are ready to serve. You can serve on the tray or transfer to large plate.

Mum's Favourite Rack of Lamb

Serves 2 People

Ingredients

Lamb rack (500g)
Gluten free wholegrain mustard
Gluten free minced garlic
Fresh rosemary
Dried Italian mixed herbs
Olive oil
Cracked black pepper

Equipment

Chopping board
Medium-sized round ceramic baking dish
Teaspoon

Note: Before you start cooking preheat your oven to 200C

Step 1. Cut your rack of lamb in half and interlock the rack bones together, making a pyramid in the middle of the baking dish. Place your fresh rosemary under the pyramid.

Step 2. Drizzle a little bit of oil on and around the lamb, and season with cracked black pepper. Add a small pinch of dried mixed Italian herbs and spread ½ a teaspoon of minced garlic over the meat. Using a teaspoon, press and rub ½ a teaspoon of gluten free wholegrain mustard on to one side of the meat, repeating the process on the other side. Your lamb is ready to be placed in the middle of your oven and roasted for 20 minutes.

Step 3. Remove from the oven and place on a heatproof surface. Season or apply more gluten free wholegrain mustard to your liking. Place back in the oven for a further 20 minutes of roasting.

Step 5. Remove from the oven and place on a heatproof surface. Cover with foil and allow to rest for 5 minutes. After 5 minutes your lamb is ready to serve with roast vegetables, potato bake or a spinach and feta salad.

Quick tip: If you like to have your lamb well done, cook for a further 10 to 15 minutes.

Louise's Roast Chicken with Gluten Free Stuffing

Serves 4 people

Ingredients

1 ½ to 2kg whole chicken
Fresh coriander
Fresh chives
1 spring onion
Cracked black pepper
Dried mixed herbs
Gluten free bread
Gluten free breadcrumbs
1 small egg
Olive oil
Gluten free minced garlic

Equipment

Tablespoon
Chopping board
Large mixing bowl
Baking tray with roasting rack

Note: Before you start cooking preheat your oven to 200C. Fill your baking tray with a small amount of water so that the rack is approximately half a centimetre above the water line.

Step 1. Toast 2 slices of gluten free bread until golden brown then remove the crusts and cut into small pieces. Place into a medium-sized mixing bowl.

Step 2. Add to the mixing bowl; 1 teaspoon of chopped fresh coriander, 1 teaspoon of chopped fresh chives, 1 chopped spring onion, 1 tablespoon of gluten free breadcrumbs, and 1 small egg. Combine by mixing with a tablespoon.

Step 3. Wash the chicken inside and out with warm water and pat dry with a paper towel. Spoon the stuffing mix into the chicken using a teaspoon, then place chicken on the roasting rack.

Step 4. Drizzle the bird with a small amount of olive oil and rub half a teaspoon of minced garlic over the chicken. Season with dried mixed herbs and cracked black pepper.

Step 5. Your chicken is ready to be placed into the oven for 1.5 to 2 hours at 200C. Once cooking, check regularly by looking through the oven door with the oven light on. Do not open the door as all the heat will escape and slow down the cook time. You are checking that the chicken is not burning; if it appears to be burning baste as per step 6. If the water in the baking tray is low or has evaporated, add a small amount of warm water. Be careful as the water can spatter when it hits the hot tray/juice. Take extreme care.

Step 6. Remove the chicken from the oven after 40 minutes and baste using the juice from the tray. You will need to do this twice while cooking.

When cooked the chicken meat will be white and if not it will be pink on the inside. Place back in oven until fully cooked and check regularly, basting the chicken to keep it moist.

Serve with vegetables such as mashed potatoes, honey carrots, potato salad, potato bake or even gluten free fried rice.

Quick tip: If you're using an outdoor kettle BBQ follow the manufacturer's instructions for warming the BBQ and cook for around 2.5 to 3 hours. You will need to check the chicken after 1.5 hours of cooking and test to see if it is cooked. If not, pop the lid back on and cook until done.

Adam's Chicken Stir-Fry

Serves 4 people

Ingredients

500g chicken breast
1 tablespoon gluten free soy sauce
1 tablespoon gluten free oyster sauce
1 tablespoon brown sugar
1 tablespoon olive oil
½ brown onion (diced)
1 teaspoon gluten free minced garlic
Cracked black pepper
1 small head of fresh broccoli
8 fresh mushrooms
Sesame seeds

Equipment

2 chopping boards
Tablespoon
Wok
Wooden spoon

Step 1. Cut the chicken into small slices and set aside. On a separate chopping board dice the mushrooms, broccoli and half of the brown onion and set aside.

Step 2. Heat a small amount of oil in your wok on a high heat. When the wok is heated add the chicken and cracked pepper and stir-fry for 3 to 4 minutes. Add the onion and stir-fry for a further 2 minutes. Add the rest of your vegetables and stir-fry for 5 minutes. You will need to stir constantly to prevent sticking and burning.

Step 3. Add 1 tablespoon each of gluten free soy sauce, gluten free oyster sauce, brown sugar and oil. Combine ingredients together and allow to simmer for 2 to 3 minutes.

Step 4. When the vegetables are cooked, turn your hot plate off, remove the wok from the heat and allow to rest before serving.

Step 5. Spoon into bowls and sprinkle with sesame seeds.

Optional extra: serve with gluten free fried rice, boiled rice or gluten free flat rice noodles.

This dish is quick and easy for a busy household.

Quick tip: You can add fresh chilli to your stir-fry for some more spice. You can leave the seeds in or remove them; it depends on how hot you would like your dish. If you use chilli flakes, try a small pinch to start with and then add more if needed.

You can substitute chicken breast for lamb or beef strips.

Pop's Rissoles and Mashed Potatoes

Serves 4 people

Ingredients

6 large potatoes
Milk
Butter
400g of beef mince
1 small egg
Gluten free breadcrumbs
Gluten free flour
Cracked pepper
Dry mixed herbs
Gluten free minced garlic
Olive oil

Equipment

Large mixing bowl
Tablespoon
Chopping board
Medium saucepan

Optional extras: Add corn on the cob with melted butter, fried onions and gluten free gravy on top of the potatoes.

Potatoes

Step 1. Half fill a medium-sized saucepan with water and put on to boil.

Step 2. Peel the potatoes and cut into quarters, placing them into the saucepan when the water reaches boiling point. Boil for 8 to 10 minutes until soft. Remove from heat and drain water from the pot.

Step 3. Using a potato masher, mash potatoes adding 1 ½ tablespoons of butter. Using a whisk, whip the potatoes and butter together and slowly add small amounts of milk. You can add as much or as little milk as you like; it depends on how thick you would like your mash.

Rissoles

Step 1. Add beef mince to a large mixing bowl and use a wooden spoon to mash and separate. Making a well in the middle of the mince, add 1 small egg, 2 tablespoons of gluten free breadcrumbs, a pinch of cracked black pepper, 2 pinches of dried mixed herbs, 1 teaspoon of gluten free minced garlic and mix together until combined.

Step 2. Using a tablespoon and your hands, spoon the mixture into one hand and roll together to make a thick patty. It should not be bigger than the palm of your hand and no thicker than 2 centimetres. Repeat step 2 until all the mixture is used.

Step 3. Heat a drizzle of oil in a pan on medium heat, rolling it around to cover the base of the pan. While the pan heats, roll your rissoles in gluten free flour.

Step 4. Place the rissoles in the heated pan and cook for around 10 minutes, turning often. Repeat steps until all rissoles are cooked. Remove from heat and allow to cool before serving.

Quick tip: Lovely vegetables to accompany this dish are corn on the cob, honey carrots, steamed broccoli, roast pumpkin, and cauliflower bake for a warm winter's night.

Sir Trent's Gluten Free Lasagne

Serves 6 people

Ingredients

600g minced beef
600g grated mozzarella cheese
300g garlic and chive flavoured cottage cheese
Mixed herbs
Cracked black pepper
Gluten free minced garlic
400g tin diced Italian tomatoes
3 tablespoons of tomato paste
1 brown onion
100g unsalted butter
1 ½ cups of milk (375ml)
Gluten free flour
Gluten free lasagna sheets (200g)
Olive oil

Equipment

Teaspoon
Tablespoon
Wooden spoon
Whisk
Ladle
Large fry pan
Small non-stick saucepan
Large oven proof baking dish (3 litre/12 cups)

Note: Before you start cooking preheat your oven to 200C.

Step 1. Drizzle a small amount of oil into the fry pan, rolling it around the base of the fry pan to coat, and place on a high heat. While the pan heats, dice half an onion into small pieces and set aside.

Step 2. Place the mince into the fry pan and cook for 10 minutes on a high heat. While cooking add a pinch of cracked black pepper, 2 teaspoons of mixed herbs, 1 teaspoon of gluten free minced garlic and the chopped onion, and stir constantly for 10 minutes.

Step 3. Turn the heat down to low and add 3 tablespoons of tomato paste and a tin of tomatoes. Stirring slowly, simmer for 5 minutes. Remove from heat and allow cooling.

Step 4. White sauce

In a small non-stick saucepan melt 100g of unsalted butter over a medium heat. Add a pinch of dried herbs and slowly whisk, adding 2 tablespoons of gluten free flour to make a paste.

Gradually add 1 ½ cups of milk, constantly whisking until smooth, moving the saucepan on and off the heat to help you work out the lumps. Once smooth remove from the heat and set aside.

Step 5. Rub the base of a baking dish with butter and half a teaspoon of minced garlic. Place 3 gluten free lasagne sheets across the base of the baking dish and cover with 2 handfuls of grated cheese, cracked pepper and 2 pinches of mixed herbs. Using a tablespoon, spoon half the mince onto the lasagne sheets and spread evenly.

Step 6. Place 3 lasagne sheets over the mince layer. Using a ladle, spoon half of the white sauce over the lasagne sheets. Spread half of the cottage cheese, 3 handfuls of grated cheese, 3 pinches of mixed herbs, cracked black pepper over top and use the rest of the minced meat.

Step 7. Place 3 more lasagne sheets over the top and cover them using the rest of the white sauce. Spread the rest of the cottage cheese over the top and use the rest of the grated cheese. Place on middle level of the oven and cook for 20 minutes. After 20 minutes remove from oven, and allow to cool before serving.

Quick tip: Serve with spinach and feta salad or steamed vegetables.

Jon's Homemade Spaghetti Bolognese

Serves 4 people

Ingredients

500g minced beef
400g tin diced Italian tomatoes
3 tablespoons tomato paste
1 teaspoon gluten free minced garlic
Cracked black pepper
2 teaspoons mixed dried herbs
1 brown onion
Olive oil
250g gluten free fettuccine pasta

Quick tip: If you need to hide vegetables for children in the bolognese sauce, use a food processer to blend them and add 1 extra small tin of diced tomatoes to hide the colour.

Equipment

Large fry pan
2 medium saucepans
Wooden spoon
Teaspoon
Tablespoon
Chopping board

Step 1. Heat large fry pan over a high heat and drizzle in a small amount of olive oil. Dice the onion and set aside. When fry pan is heated add the minced meat to the pan, stirring constantly for 3 minutes. After 3 minutes add the onion to the pan and keep stirring. Season with cracked black pepper, 1 teaspoon of minced garlic and 2 teaspoons of mixed dried herbs and cook for a further 5 minutes until meat has browned. Remove fry pan from the heat.

Step 2. Place a small amount of olive oil in one of the medium-sized saucepans and place on a low heat to warm. Once warm, transfer the mince into this saucepan.

Step 3. Add 3 tablespoons of tomato paste and a 400g tin of diced Italian tomatoes and mix together, placing the lid on top to simmer for 20 minutes. Stir 3 to 4 times or when needed.

Step 4. Half fill a medium-sized saucepan with water and bring to the boil. Add 250g of gluten free fettuccine pasta to the saucepan, stirring when needed. Cook for 8 to 10 minutes or until desired texture is reached. Remove from heat and drain pasta into a strainer then rinse with hot water. Place bolognese and pasta in a bowl and you're ready to serve.

Quick tip: Serve with grated vintage cheese, grated mozzarella cheese or parmesan cheese. It's also nice with gluten free garlic bread or spinach and feta salad.

Cooper's Chicken Bites

Serves 4 people

Ingredients

500g chicken breast
1 large egg (whisked)
¼ cup gluten free flour
½ cup gluten free bread crumbs
2 teaspoons gluten free Moroccan seasoning
Olive oil

Equipment

Chopping board
3 bowls
2 plates
Wok
Paper towels

Step 1. Trim chicken, cut into bite size pieces and place on a clean plate.

Step 2. Add ¼ cup of gluten free flour to a bowl and set aside. Whisk 1 egg in the next bowl and set aside. Add ½ cup of gluten free breadcrumbs and 2 teaspoons of Moroccan seasoning to the last bowl, mix together and set aside. Place dishes in a line starting with the chicken, then the gluten free flour, then the whisked egg, and lastly the gluten free bread crumbs bowl. Place a clean plate at the end of the line for the completed crumbed chicken.

Step 3. Roll and press chicken into the gluten free flour, then dip into the whisked egg and coat all over. Next, roll and press the chicken into the gluten free breadcrumbs, ensuring it is evenly covered. Repeat these steps until all the chicken is crumbed.

Step 4. Fill the wok with 2 cups of olive oil, and warm on a medium heat. When the oil is hot, add 4 to 5 pieces of chicken to the oil and cook for 2 to 3 minutes on each side. When cooked, the chicken will be firm and golden brown. Remove from the oil and place on a paper towel to dry. Repeat until all the chicken is cooked. Your chicken is now ready to serve.

Quick tip: These chicken bites work well with potato bake, potato salad, fried rice, steamed vegetables, mashed potato or spinach and feta salad. Try dipping in gluten free sweet chilli sauce, mango chutney, gluten free smoky BBQ sauce or, a mix of sour cream and sweet chilli sauce.

Eagle Pond's Roast Salmon

Serves 2 people

Ingredients

2 salmon fillets (250g each)
2 spring onions
¼ cup diced red capsicum
¼ cup diced green capsicum
Avocado oil
White vinegar
Cracked black pepper
Dried Italian herbs
Lemon juice

Equipment

Chopping board
Foil
Baking paper
Baking tray
Medium-sized bowl

Note: Before you start cooking, preheat your oven to 200C.

Step 1. Cover the baking tray with baking paper. Cut 2 pieces of foil big enough to wrap the salmon in, and place them on the baking tray.

Clean the salmon and place each piece skin side down on top of each piece of foil. Fold foil around the base of the salmon fillets, leaving the top open.

Step 2. Drizzle a small amount of olive oil and white vinegar over the salmon. Chop 2 spring onions into small pieces and evenly sprinkle over the top of the salmon with the diced red and green capsicum. Season with cracked black pepper, mixed dried herbs and a few drops of lemon juice.

Step 3. Fold the foil around the salmon to cover, then press and fold the edges together to seal. Place in oven and bake for 20 minutes. After 20 minutes remove from the oven and check the salmon – it should start to turn white inside. Place back in the oven for a further 20 minutes until salmon is cooked through. The salmon will be white all the way through when cooked. Remove from oven and open the foil carefully. Allow to cool before serving.

Quick tip: Serve with potato salad, spinach and feta salad or mashed potato and steamed honey carrots.

Oak Street's Smashed Avo Burgers

Makes 6-8 Burgers

Ingredients

600g minced meat
10 rashers smoky bacon
1 egg
Butter
1 tablespoon gluten free corn flour
1 teaspoon fresh garlic chives
½ teaspoon gluten free minced garlic
2 tomatoes
2 large brown onions
1 fresh ripe avocado
Lemon juice
Cracked black pepper
Pinch of salt
1 teaspoon dried herbs
Gluten free mayonnaise
Sliced cheese
Washed spinach leaves
6-8 gluten free burger buns, corn wraps, sandwich buns or pita bread

Equipment

Large mixing bowl
Small mixing bowl
Chopping board
Grater
Tongs
Spatula

Step 1. Place minced meat into the large mixing bowl, separate and make a well in the middle of the meat. Add 1 teaspoon of chopped fresh garlic chives, ½ teaspoon of minced garlic, 1 tablespoon of corn flour, 1 teaspoon of mixed herbs and 2 pinches of cracked black pepper. Add 1 egg to the mixture and mix using a wooden spoon.

Step 2. Cut and de-seed 1 avocado. Place the avocado flesh into a clean small bowl and mash. Add 1 pinch of salt and 5 drops of lemon juice, continuing to mash and mix until smooth. Set aside.

Step 3. Take the mince mixture and make patties the size of the palm of your hand. Shape them in a circle or oval depending on the shape of the burger buns, bread or wraps. Repeat until all the mixture is used.

Step 4. Heat a BBQ plate on and dice the onions ready to fry. When heated, place the patties on the BBQ plate and cook for 8 to 10 minutes. After 5 minutes place the smoky bacon rashers on the BBQ plate with onions. Add 1 teaspoon of butter to the onions and cook for 5 minutes. Remove and turn off BBQ.

Note: To check if your meat patties are cooked cut one open, the meat will not be pink if it is cooked.

Step 5. If desired, toast your gluten free burger buns or bread. Then spread on the smashed avocado, adding spinach leaves, sliced tomato, mayonnaise and cheese as desired. Top with the meat patty, bacon and onion and your burger is ready to eat.

Quick tip: If you need to remove the egg from the patty mix, replace it with 1 tablespoon of gluten free corn flour to help bind the patty together. For an egg free version do not use mayonnaise. You can also change the cheese to lactose-free grated cheese and use dairy free butter.

Sweet Treats

Fleur's Chocolate Mousse

Serves 6

Ingredients

250ml thickened cream
400g gluten free chocolate
Salt
Gluten free cocoa powder
Strawberries
Whipped cream
Water

Equipment

Large mixing bowl
Electric beater
Wine glasses x 6
Spatula
Tablespoon
Teaspoon
Sharp knife
A large measuring jug
Wooden spoon
Small pot
Small heat-proof glass bowl

Step 1. Using the electric beater whip the thickened cream until it forms soft peaks and then set aside.

Step 2. Fill the small pot ¼ full of water and bring to the boil. Place heat-proof bowl over the top of the pot, making sure that the bowl is not touching the water.

Step 3. Break the chocolate into small bits and place it into the bowl, mixing with a metal spoon until the chocolate has melted. Mix slowly and add small amounts at a time until all the chocolate has been added. Remove from heat.

Step 4. Using a spatula, fold the melted chocolate into the cream. Gradually add 1 teaspoon of cocoa powder to the mixture with a pinch of salt then combine all together.

Step 5. Spoon the mixture into the large measuring jug and pour into wine glasses. Place into the fridge for 3 to 4 hours to set before serving.

Quick tip: When serving use whipped cream and cut a strawberry in half to place on top. Try it with shaved chocolate on top!

Sparkle's Apple Chocolate Muffins

Ingredients

1½ cups gluten free self-raising flour
1 tablespoon gluten free coconut flour
1 teaspoon gluten free bicarbonate soda
1 teaspoon vanilla essence
½ cup brown sugar
1 egg (beaten)
2 tablespoons honey
150ml milk
50g unsalted butter (melted)
1 cup gluten free chocolate chips
1 small green apple (peeled and thinly sliced)

Equipment

Measuring cups
Tablespoon
Teaspoon
Whisk
Wooden spoon
Measuring jug
Chopping board
Large mixing bowl
Small mixing bowl
Cooling rack
Muffin tin

Note: Preheat your oven to 200C before you start cooking.

Step 1. Place 1½ cups of gluten free flour, ½ cup of brown sugar, 1 tablespoon of coconut flour, 1 teaspoon of bicarbonate soda and 1 teaspoon of vanilla essence into a large mixing bowl and combine.

Step 2. Beat 1 egg. Make a well in the flour mixture and add the egg to the middle of the well. Add 150ml of milk, 1 cup of gluten free chocolate chips, 2 tablespoons of honey and mix together.

Step 3. Melt 50 grams of unsalted butter in the microwave for about 1 minute and 15 seconds, and add to the mixture. Peel and thinly slice the apple and then cut into small pieces to your liking. Add to mixture and mix for 2 minutes.

Step 4. Using a paper towel, grease all muffin tins with butter. Using a tablespoon, spoon the mixture into the muffin tins until ¾ full. Place in the middle of the oven for about 15 to 20 minutes. After 10 minutes have a sneaky peek at your muffins by turning on the oven light, as you may need to rotate your muffin tin so that all the muffins bake evenly. After 15 minutes remove the muffins from the oven and test them to see if they are cooked. Pierce a skewer in the middle of the muffin and if it comes out clean, your muffins are cooked. You could also test your muffins by tapping the top of the muffin and if it bounces back with no batter on your finger, it's cooked.

Quick tip: You can change the milk to a substitute of your choice, such as skim, soy, rice or goat's milk. You can also use soy, dark, milk, or dairy free chocolate, or for something different try caramel and chocolate drops. If you cook the muffins for 20 minutes they will be crunchy on the outside and soft on the inside.

5th Avenue's Chocolate Rose Cake

Ingredients

1½ cups gluten free flour
½ cup water
2 to 3 ripe bananas
2 tablespoons honey
½ cup brown sugar
100g unsalted butter (melted)
1 egg (whisked)
1 teaspoon gluten free bicarbonate soda
1 teaspoon vanilla essence
½ teaspoon gluten free baking cocoa

Equipment

Measuring cups
Tablespoon
Teaspoon
Fork
Medium round cake tin
2 large mixing bowls, with a lip if possible
Wooden spoon
Cooling rack

Step 1. Preheat oven to 200C. Using a paper towel, grease the cake tin with butter and set aside.

Step 2. Using a fork, mash the bananas in the mixing bowl. Add 1½ cups of gluten free flour, 1 teaspoon of baking soda, ½ a cup of sugar and stir together with the banana. Make a well in the middle of the mixture and add 1 whisked egg, ½ a cup of water, 100g of melted butter, 2 tablespoons of honey, 1 teaspoon of vanilla essence and stir to combine. You will need to stir for around 2 minutes to get all the lumps out of the mixture.

Step 3. Halve the mixture evenly into two mixing bowls. Set one bowl aside. Add cocoa to the other mixture and stir through.

Step 4. Pour a 10cm circle of the cocoa mixture into the middle of the cake tin and stop. Change mixtures and pour the light mixture into the middle of the cocoa mixture to make a smaller circle and then stop. Repeat until all of the mixture is used.

Step 5. Place in oven for 35 to 45 minutes. To check if the cake is cooked, pierce the middle of the cake with a skewer. If it comes out clean, your cake is ready. Remove the cake from the cake tin and place onto a cooling rack for 10 to 15 minutes before serving.

Quick tip: The chocolate rose cake tastes nice with vanilla icing for a lovely afternoon tea with friends.

Julie Ann's Rocky Road

Note: Before you start cooking, line a slice tray with baking paper and set aside.

Step 1. In a large mixing bowl, combine coconut, gluten free marshmallows, roasted hazelnuts, flaked almonds, and gluten free gummy lollies. Combine the ingredients by gently mixing.

Step 2. Using a microwave safe bowl, melt the chocolate in a microwave on the low setting, stirring every 30 seconds.

Step 3. When the chocolate has melted remove from microwave and add it to the lolly mixture, mixing to combine.

Step 4. Pour and flatten the combined mixture into your slice tray and evenly spread it across the tray. Place in the refrigerator for 2 hours to set.

Step 5. Remove from fridge and cut into slices.

Your Rocky Road is now ready to serve.

Quick tip: You can remove the nuts from this recipe if needed and add more gluten free lollies.

Ingredients

300g gluten free milk cooking chocolate (optional change to soy or organic chocolate)
1 cup gluten free dessicated coconut
150g gluten free marshmallows
200g roasted hazelnuts
50g flaked almonds
100g gluten free gummy lollies

Equipment

1 cup
Large mixing bowl
Baking paper
Slice tray
Wooden spoon
Small saucepan

Chorleywood's Banana Bread

Ingredients

1½ cups gluten free self-raising flour
3 ripe bananas
½ cup raw sugar
2 tablespoons honey
1 large egg (beaten)
1/3 cup unsalted butter (melted)
1 teaspoon vanilla essence
1 teaspoon gluten free bicarbonate soda
Pinch of salt
100ml milk
Butter

Equipment

Measuring cups
Teaspoon
Tablespoon
Large mixing bowl
Small mixing bowl
Microwave heatproof bowl
Whisk
Wooden spoon
Measuring jug
Loaf tin

Note: Before you start cooking preheat your oven to 200C.

Step 1. In a large mixing bowl combine 1½ cups of gluten free flour, ½ cup of raw sugar, 1 teaspoon of gluten free bicarbonate soda, a pinch of salt and mix ingredients together.

Step 2. In a small mixing bowl, mash the bananas together with 1 teaspoon of vanilla essence. Add to the large mixing bowl and mix all ingredients together.

Step 3. Make a well in the middle of the mixture. Melt 1/3 cup of butter in a microwave safe bowl and add to mixture. Add 2 tablespoons of honey, 100ml of milk and 1 beaten egg to the mixture. Mix all ingredients together for 2 minutes.

Step 4. Grease loaf tin using a paper towel and butter. Pour the mixture into the baking tin and bake for 35 minutes at 200C.

Step 5. Remove from oven and test your banana bread by piercing the middle with a skewer. If it comes out clean, your cake is cooked. Place on a cooling rack for 10 to 15 minutes before serving.

Quick tip: Banana bread is nice for children's lunch boxes for morning tea or a tasty treat for when they get home from school. Banana bread is quick and easy to prepare for unexpected visitors and goes well with a nice cup of tea. If you have a flat sandwich press you can toast a thick slice for a warm crisp treat.

Jenny's Blueberry Cake

Ingredients

2 tablespoons gluten free blueberry jam
2 cups gluten free flour
150ml of milk
1 small egg (beaten)
1 teaspoon gluten free bicarbonate soda
½ cup raw sugar
1½ cups gluten free chocolate chips
50g melted better
125g fresh blueberries

Quick tip: If you have a sweet tooth and would like to make it a dessert cake add 1 tablespoon of fresh honey and serve warm with gluten free vanilla ice cream or whipped cream, with chocolate shavings to go on top.

You can also change the milk and chocolate to soy products if needed and it will still taste great.

Equipment

Large mixing bowl
Wooden spoon
Measuring jug
Tablespoon
Teaspoon
Cake tin size 8 inch round
Cake rack

Note: Before you start cooking preheat your oven to 200C.

Step 1. To your mixing bowl add 2 cups of gluten free flour, ½ cup of sugar, 1 teaspoon of bicarbonate soda, 1½ cups of gluten free chocolate chips and 125g of fresh blueberries. Mix gently together and set aside.

Step 2. Melt 50g butter in the microwave for 1 minute. Make a well in the blueberry mixture and pour in the melted butter. Add 2 tablespoons of gluten free blueberry jam. Whisk 1 egg in a small bowl then add to the well in the mix. Using your measuring jug measure out 150ml of milk and gently pour it into the mixture. Slowly combine all ingredients using a wooden spoon, mixing and folding together for around 1 minute.

Step 3. Grease your cake tin with butter using paper towel, rubbing it around the inside of the tin. Pour the mixture into the cake tin and place in the oven for 25 minutes at 200C.

Step 4. After 25 minutes, turn the oven down to 150C, rotate the cake tin and bake for a further 25 minutes.

Step 5. After 25 minutes at 150C, remove cake from the oven. Check if your cake is cooked by piercing with a skewer in the middle and side of the cake. If it comes out clean then your cake is ready. Place cake on cooling rack for 5 to 10 minutes before serving.

Spring Mountains Pancakes

Makes 6 to 8 medium (10-15cm) sized pancakes

Ingredients

1 cup gluten free self-raising flour
300ml milk
1 tablespoon gluten free coconut flour
1 teaspoon vanilla essence
1 small banana

Quick tip: You can use soy milk if needed.

Equipment

Large mixing bowl
1 cup
Tablespoon
Teaspoon
Whisk
Non-stick spatula to flip pancake
Measuring jug
Large fry pan

Step 1. To a large mixing bowl add 1 cup of gluten free self-raising flour and 1 tablespoon of gluten free coconut flour. Stir together and make a well in the middle.

Step 2. Measure out and add 300ml of milk to the mixture and start whisking. Add 1 teaspoon of vanilla essence and whisk all ingredients together until smooth. Set aside for 5 minutes.

Step 3. Heat a large frying pan on a medium heat and add a little butter to the pan. Distribute the butter evenly by swirling to coat the base of the fry pan. Slice banana into small thin slices and set aside until needed. When the fry pan is heated pour the batter into the middle of the fry pan to make a circle around 10-15cm wide. After the batter has started to bubble, place banana slices on top and gently press into the pancake.

Step 4. Cook for 2-3 minutes, until bubbles appear on top of pancake. Turn and cook for a further 1-2 minutes. Stack pancakes on top of each other to keep warm and repeat steps until batter is finished.

Quick tip: You can serve your gluten free pancakes topped with gluten free vanilla ice cream or soy ice cream, whipped cream, strawberries and honey.

You can serve pancakes for snacks, breakfast, and brunch or for dessert.

Sometimes they're nice to put in children's lunchboxes for a sweet treat, served with strawberry jam in the middle.

Bear Trap's Orange and Almond Muffins

Ingredients

1 cup gluten free flour
½ cup gluten free quinoa flour
¾ cup caster sugar
1 teaspoon gluten free bicarbonate soda
½ cup flaked almonds
Pinch of salt
125g unsalted butter (melted)
1 egg (beaten)
80ml orange juice
2 tablespoons gluten free orange marmalade
2 teaspoons orange zest (1 small orange)

Equipment

Teaspoon
Tablespoon
Wooden spoon
Measuring jug
Whisk
Large mixing bowl
Measuring cups
Grater
Cooling rack
Microwave safe dish
Muffin tin

Note: Before you start cooking, preheat your oven to 200C and grease your muffin tin with butter.

Step 1. In a large mixing bowl combine 1 cup of gluten free flour, ½ cup of gluten free quinoa flour, ¾ of a cup of caster sugar, 1 teaspoon of bicarbonate soda, a pinch of salt and ½ cup of flaked almonds and mix together. Make a well in the middle of the mixture after mixing.

Step 2. Using a microwave safe bowl, melt 125g of unsalted butter for 1 minute in the microwave and add to middle of the well. Also add to the well 80ml of orange juice, 1 beaten egg and 2 tablespoons of gluten free orange marmalade. Grate 2 tablespoons of orange zest to add to the well, then combine the ingredients, mixing for 2 minutes.

Step 3. Fill the muffin tins ¾ full, so the mixture won't overflow when rising. Place into the middle of the oven for about 15 to 20 minutes. After 10 minutes have a sneaky peek at your muffins by turning on the oven light, as you may need to rotate your muffin tin for even baking. After 15 minutes remove the muffins from the oven and test to see if they are cooked. Pierce the middle of a muffin with a skewer and if it comes out clean, your muffins are cooked. You could also test your muffins by tapping the top of the muffin; if it bounces back with no batter on your finger, it's cooked.

Quick tip: You can change the milk to a substitute of your liking such as skim, soy, rice or goat's milk.

Nan's Short Bread

Ingredients

250g unsalted butter
2 cups caster sugar
5 eggs
1 egg white for baking glaze
1 teaspoon gluten free baking powder
1 teaspoon gluten free baking soda
1 teaspoon vanilla essence
¼ cup milk
Pinch of salt
750g gluten free flour
1 cup gluten free corn flour

Equipment

2 large mixing bowls
Small heatproof bowl
Measuring cups
Teaspoon
Fork
Wooden spoon
Whisk
Cooking brush
Cookie cutters
Cooling rack

Note: Before you start cooking preheat your oven to 150C.

Step 1. Melt the butter in the microwave on high and add to a large bowl. Slowly add 5 eggs one by one and mix together slowly with a whisk. Add 1 teaspoon of vanilla essence and ¼ cup of milk to the mixture, combining all of the ingredients together using a whisk. Using a tablespoon add the sugar slowly, mixing as you go. Set aside.

Step 2. In the other mixing bowl add 750g of gluten free flour, 1 cup of corn flour, 1 teaspoon of baking powder, 1 teaspoon of baking soda and a pinch of salt, and mix together with a wooden spoon. Make a well in the middle of the mixture and add the wet ingredients, mixing so it starts to form a dough in the bowl.

Step 3. At this point you can start using your hands to knead the dough. Dust a clean surface with gluten free flour. Place the dough on the surface and start kneading. After the dough has formed and has made a large ball, dust with gluten free flour and place in a clean mixing bowl. Cover with cling wrap and place in refrigerator for 10 minutes.

Step 4. Dust your clean surface with a small amount of gluten free flour so the dough doesn't stick. Remove the dough from the refrigerator after 10 minutes and roll out the dough with a rolling pin to a thickness of approximately 1cm. Then start to cut your cookies with the cookie cutters. If you don't have cookie cutters you can form twist, plaits, circles and fancy shapes. You can also roll into small balls and use a fork to push the top down so it flattens the short bread.

Step 5. Brush cookies with egg whites for a golden glow. Place in the oven for 10 to 15 minutes. Keep a close eye on your cookies while they are baking as they may need to be rotated to cook evenly.

Step 6. Remove from the oven. Your cookies should end up looking firm with a nice golden glow. Place on a cooling rack for 10 minutes before serving.

Quick tip: You can serve these cookies with jam and whipped cream while having a lovely cup of tea.

Notes

www.ingramcontent.com/pod-product-compliance
Ingram Content Group UK Ltd.
Pitfield, Milton Keynes, MK11 3LW, UK
UKHW060117300726
14090UKWH00002B/243
9780994176745